MW00976832

Interlochen Public Library
9700 Riley Road
Interlochen MI  49643

# LIGHT
## AS A
# FEATHER

# LIGHT
# AS A
# FEATHER

◆

*Written and Illustrated*

*by*

## Lissi Kaplan

Little Finch Press

FIRST EDITION

All rights reserved, including the right of reproduction in whole or in part in any form.

Copyright © 2016 by Lissi Kaplan

Published by

Little Finch Press

P.O. Box 1110

Agoura Hills, CA 91376

www.littlefinchpress.com

Manufactured in the United States of America

ISBN 978-0-692-75463-4

Cover and interior design by Sheila Hart Design, Inc.

For my precious grandchildren,

who inspire the magic inside of me

and allow my spirit to take flight…

May you always be true to your own song.

# ACKNOWLEDGMENTS

Writing a story this personal, I was blessed to have met Michael Wilde, an extraordinarily gifted editor. Michael took my story and delicately and lovingly honored each word. He turned *Light as a Feather* into a piece of art. I thank you, Michael.

My children, Scott, Michelle, and Aaron, we have been on a journey of life together. My love for you is beyond description, art, or words.

Doug, my love and dear friend, thank you for being by my side and encouraging me to get my book out into the universe.

Sindi and Beth, my sisters, my heart, you are my greatest support in everything I dream about.

Laura Ross, thank you for reading my manuscript and using your editorial skills, direction, and poetic talents to take this project to completion.

Sheila Hart, my talented book designer, thank you for your passionate input and for listening to my vision and taking it to an ethereal level of sheer magic.

# LIGHT
## AS A
# FEATHER

# PREFACE

———◆———

*Light as a Feather* is based in part on a true story. Many springs ago, I was faced with one of life's difficult challenges, and was desperately trying to find my inner peace and joy again. While I was painting in my kitchen studio each day, a little brown wren tapped at the outside of my window persistently, until I was forced to get up and look him in the eye. The bird would dance, flap his wings, and do somersaults over and over again, trying to communicate with me. This went on for several months until one day, he left and never returned.

Soon after, two new birds came to me and began making the same effort, tapping and dancing at the same kitchen window. I started looking forward to the early morning tapping-and-dancing game in my studio and it slowly transformed me—and lifted my spirits. I started feeling lighter and more joyful again.

I know in my heart that the tenacity and loving friendship of those birds helped me find my way back to myself. And over time, as I healed, the seeds of this story were planted, took root, and blossomed into the book you are now holding. The birds inspired me to continue doing the work that nourishes my soul and brings me joy. I now think of them fondly as my spirit guides.

I offer you this book with deep appreciation to Lady Dry Feather, Tender Wing, and Wise Wing.

*L.K.*
*Calabasas, California*
*August 2016*

# 1

Little Feather was called just that the minute he broke from his shell.

"He's even little for a wren," said Momma Bird, "and he weighs no more than a feather."

"Truer than true!" Poppa Bird sang, feeding the baby a worm. "This so you may grow, and fly someday, like my father and his grandfathers, too."

"And grandmothers," Momma Bird joined in, "whose songs we carry when we take wing."

"Yes! Fly is what I wanna do! And sing!"

"Not yet," Momma and Poppa cooed.

"Then when?" the little wren cried.

"All in its time," Momma Bird replied.

Poppa Bird added, "Soon."

The baby was bursting with excitement.

"When, oh when?" Little Feather couldn't stop.

"If you try to fly now," both of them cautioned,

"you'll drop."

All that day,

he wiggled and waggled,

pulling this way and that way

testing the nest.

At first, he listed and rolled to his side

then he turned and he twisted—

and almost fell—

flopping back down to rest.

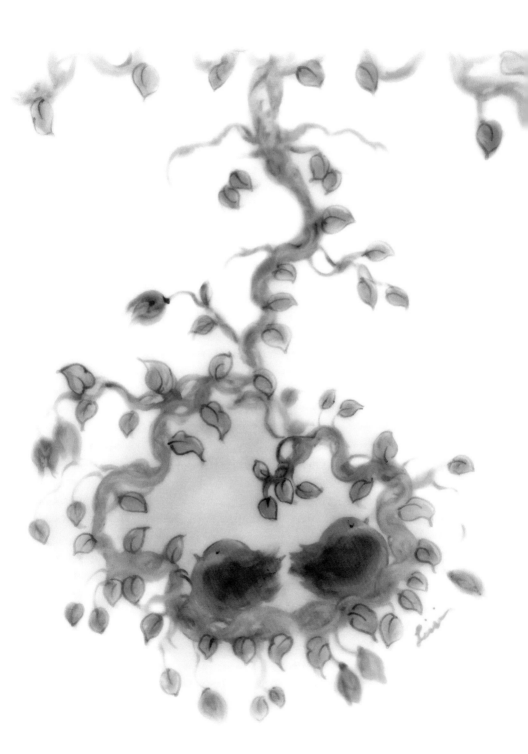

At night,

Momma Bird sang her baby to sleep

with songs of dream birds whose spirits flew far,

of life and love and all of the things

that happen when little birds first take wing.

Some of the stories made Little Feather laugh,

some made him tremble and cry;

some made him yearn to be everything more;

all of them made him wish he could fly.

Now he closes his eyes to sleep

and dreams of songs his grandfathers sang

of faraway places and setting suns,

crimson moons, vermilion seas;

of silvery peacock mountaintops

indigo skies and raw umber trees.

He dreamed of thick sienna woods

and flies through canopies speckled green,

through shadows, lamp and ivory black,

over rippling rivers of ultramarine.

Restless, soaring through the night

Little Feather's spirit took flight.

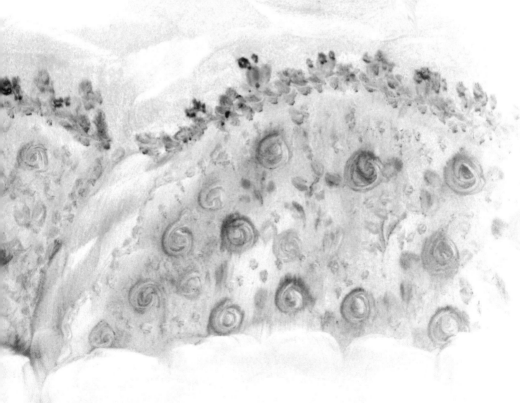

# 2

Morning cracked the lemon sun

and gave the little bird heart.

He'd practiced all his skills for weeks:

lighting on the slimmest branch,

balancing on a reed;

venturing bit by bit from the nest,

hazarding a start

until, at last, Little Feather was ready.

The songs, he explained to

his momma and poppa,

of that faraway place in his dreams

were calling.

"They sing in colors, shades and hues,

and speak in different voices."

Momma and Poppa Bird looked at each other

and knew the time had come.

"Little Feather," they said, "you've been

given a spirit

and life, and precious breath.

Go fly

and soar

and find new things"—

each touched one of the tiny bird's wings—

"and remember to love

and be happy."

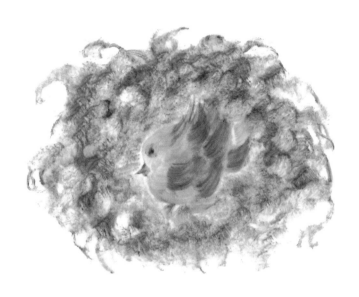

# 3

Flying through that bright hot day

and stopping only once for a grub,

Little Feather spotted a patch of shade

and gathered up sticks in the brambly scrub.

With twigs and reeds and blades of grass,

he built his nest among the leaves

well hidden in a prickly shrub.

Hopping along the ground

he tested the weeds with his slender bill

for bugs, and having had his fill

Little Feather nestled down

as yellow day turned orange-brown.

Alone, that night,

the little wren awoke in fright:

Staring back, a foot away

were a pair of shining eyes.

*A rat!*

It sat in the shadows and barely twitched,

studying him

as *prey*.


Then with a howl and terrifying shriek

a long-eared owl came swooping in

and carried the rat off in its beak.

Little Feather shuddered, rattled with fear

by things in the night that you can't see or hear.

He turned and tossed

imagining snakes

winding through brush;

when he thought of them sliding under wet leaves,

he felt lonely and hopeless,

all courage lost

and from that moment on

the night felt bewitched.

Daybreak couldn't come too soon.

He woke up safe and sound in his nest

listening to a song:

*oozeeee delzeedle-eedle-ooh*

*tse tetetetete*

*zrink zrink!*

This was followed by a soft dry *chrrr*

and a very sharp *jik!*

"Where are you, please, and who?" he cried.

A bird lighted next to him

aflurry and aflutter

with translucent wings.


"I couldn't help but notice the wistful note

in every bright color you sing."

"Too true!" he rued. "My first time away,

I don't think I'm ready and now I'm afraid."

"Understandably so," Lady Dry Feather cooed.

"Allow me,"

she extended the tip of her toe

to make more room on the twig.


"I didn't see how impossibly hard it could be,"

the little wren continued,

"and I'm heavy with doubt."

"Fire your heart with faith. You'll see,"

said the wren's new friend, impenetrably.

"And remember not to be too quick

to punish yourself for being too thick

or hard on yourself for not being strong

and be willing enough to admit when you're wrong."

Lady Dry Feather blinked, and followed this speech

with a soft *wijo* and *twee pudo twee tweep*.

"May I ask a question?"

"Of course."

"How soon will I know what message to carry?

What wisdom

what words

from ancestor birds?

Their mystery dreams of faraway lands

send me to places I don't understand."


"You remind me of me," Lady Dry Feather sighed.

Then she drew close, with a daring eye.

"You will know

the ebb and flow

of earth and water,

wind and trees

A heart to beat

a sky to touch

how all can be a part of one

how one apart can fall

How love is life

and also grief

that suffers every joy

That darkness cools unsettled night;

how precious light is brief."

Little Feather paused. A lot to consider.

"One more thing," Lady Dry Feather added

with spirit.

"Try not to worry too much."

# 4

The more Little Feather flew the more he grew

until he attained what knowledge he could

to go about simply, to carry a breeze

on his wings

from the roots to the top of the trees.

*This isn't enough, there has to be more,* he mused,

*for me to be ready.*

The time had come, he knew, to leave the woods.

# 5

*Tap tap.*

*Tap tap.*

The sad-looking woman set down her teacup

and quietly moved her chair closer.

On the other side of the windowpane

her tiny guest sang a soft refrain.

*Tea-kettle tea-kettle tea-kettle*

"Would you like some? I'm afraid it's too hot,"

said the woman with eyes and a voice filled

with rain.

The bird erupted into bubbling cheer:

high, clear descending notes

ending with a drawn-out *zheeeer*

*Kit-kit!*

and for a brief moment grief lifted a bit.

Each day,

during afternoon Tapping Game tea

half-empty sadness

melted away

The little wren's rapping on

her window glass

bound them together as sea and sky

with a sun and moon who seemed to cry,

"This too shall pass!"

# 6

One morning, having just returned from a house

Little Feather heard a low burble

a warbling *jree*

then *tutututututu tweedle t-t zree!*

*What is it?* he wondered, cocking one ear.

*How captivating! What style!* Little Feather

marveled.

He tried calling back with an improvised *zrink*

but sounded as though he were choking

on marbles.

"This is shocking!" he gasped.

He flicked up his tail.

"What could possibly be the matter?"

He opened his bill and all that came out

was a feeble wheeze and buzzing chatter.

He scrabbled the dirt and ruffed his wing

then hopped on a branch and attempted to sing.

*Tsik! T–t t–t t–t jirt!*

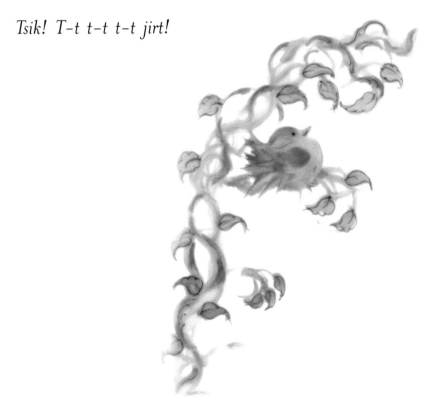

"That doesn't sound right,"

came a voice from above.

"Who thinks so?" said Little Feather,

searching the sky.

He listened to the trees and heard only quiet.

Still, echoes of that earlier call

lingered sweetly in his ear.


So he puffed up his chest and tried to reply—

but all he could manage was a single *zweeeer.*

"Your buzzer is off," the voice continued.

"No one understands you."

Little Feather kicked and cried, *"Who cares!"*

"Such a pronouncement. A shame."

"Besides," the little bird flamed,

"I've tried and tried and tried. I give up!"

His outburst was followed by silence.

After an eternity, the voice at last replied.

"For a fledgling, it's certainly a tough way to go."

"You don't know!"

"I do."

"Well then, who are you?"

"You might call me Tender Wing;

or you may not, depending..."

"Depending on what?"

"It isn't for me to answer."

"Why can't I see you?"

"Who says you can't?"

"I'm talking to the sky and I only see trees."

"Then take a look at the forest."

The riddle seemed to stump the wren.

Frustration grew and grew;

then turned to rage, a lashing out

at everything he thought he knew

and loved

until he stumbled off his perch

and tumbled into a puddle of pity headfirst.

"That's not the way to find out why or who,"

the gentle voice suggested,

"never mind the what or how."

Little Feather splashed about his muddle

and managed to cease his blubbering.

Something about that voice was familiar,

something from his ancestor dreams

urging him now to carry his feelings

to others

recalling his heart to sing.

He felt brighter.

"I remember!" Little Feather sprouted to his feet.

Churring a musical *tew-tew-tew-tew*

he banished that lonely self-pity and fear:

with a hearty *cheee-wee* and the faith of a fighter

he *ootled* and *keetled*

and rising in song,

worked himself up to an explosive *Kit! Kit!*

What Little Feather didn't yet know

was that far, far off his call had been heard ...

until, from a distant grove came a cheery

*Pidaro! Pidaro! Pidaro!*

# 7

Little Feather had found his soul mate—

Little Sweet Feather, whose melody

woke in him a joy

to build their happy nest—

and soon-to-be *nestling's* home.

After a turn of the smiling moon

the hatchling broke from her shell:

her blue took on a pinkish hue

that grew to be a lovely plume

and together they named her Little Pink Feather.


Before too long, she started making noises,

mostly peeps and little rasps.

While the brand-new momma protected her baby

Little Feather foraged for beetles and wasps.

Sometimes, during these flights from the nest

his heart would follow his spirit away

to unseen places, distant elms

and oaks

where ancestor songbirds dwelled.

He sought the truth

the timeless words

of ruby-throated hummingbirds

whose restless, never-ending flight

called to him in dreams.

That night, he confided to Little Sweet Feather

his desire to answer the spirit call

that guided him to carry a melody

not yet sung in his heart.


"And for that," he insisted with urgency,

"I must seek the source of mystery,

the source of our calling: the ancestor tree."

Little Pink Feather, pretending to sleep,

overheard their conversation

and begged to know more.

"If I knew," Little Feather answered her plea,

"I'd know the difference between pink and blue—

and where and why and how and who—

without flying the distance between them, to grow."

The baby looked confused.

"My own Poppa Bird explained to me once

how wisdom isn't just words;

when we fly, we carry ourselves, our feelings."

Little Pink Feather smiled.

"I want to carry my feelings too! Right now!"

"Not yet," said Momma Bird, "but soon,

your dreams will show you how."

"But when?" the baby bird cried loud.

"You'll know."

"When? Oh, when is that?"

"The next time, when I see you," Little Feather

replied.

"Now best get back to sleep."

# 8

Little Feather listened to the nighttime sounds

of the forest, not at all afraid.

His song was calling through memory's dreamscape

across ancient oceans and petrified time;

it sang in a chain of unbroken voices

deep in the midnight surround.

This was the sign, from when he was small

before he had learned to heavily sigh;

now he needed to carry his riddle to the source—

so he hopped off the branch and flew.

And he flew

and flew and flew

and flew and flew and flew.

Tired and weary

thirsty, bleary

the little wren landed on a massive oak.


He was struck by the strength

and length of its beauty.

Knotty bumps and knobby gnarls

ran up and down like stepping-stones,

inviting any passing through

to settle on a bough.


"Ancient Lady!" Little Feather recognized at once.

"Your shady arms have beckoned me

across a sea of time and space,

to help me carry a dreaming song

and to solve the riddle of fear and faith!"

A portal opened wide:

deep within, a voice replied,

"Someone else is here."

A hummingbird descended.

"Follow the lights of the fireflies

to help you see," the bird advised

then just as quickly, zipped away.

*How strange*, Little Feather thought.

*I've been here before, but I don't recall*

*having seen such a brilliant fluorescent display.*

A swirling array of wings

glowed bright

and twirled him deeper in.

With every bend and loving curl

the wren felt lighter and lighter;

a peaceful calm enveloped him

in radiant iridescence.

Through delicate layers of fireflies

a pair of looming luminous eyes

peered from unseen depths of the tree.


"Come ... sit by me, open your heart,"

urged a voice from the ancient well.


"There are days," Little Feather began,

"that I feel that I'm sinking—

when everything weighs too much.

That I've lost what I know,

and all of my thinking

has left me,

without a message to carry,

empty and alone."

"I suppose … you'd like to know why,"

said Wise Wing.

Little Feather held back tears.

"Close your eyes and look back," the old bird

continued.

"Concentrate hard. Tell me what you see."

*Momma Bird and Poppa Bird …*

Wise Wing added, "nurturing you for your very

first flight."

*Little Sweet Feather …*

"Always close by."

*Little Pink Feather …* Little Feather thought raptly.

"Wrapped in your arms each night. Go on."

*Lady Dry Feather ...*

"Your first spirit bird, helping you fire your

courage with faith."

*And that together, alive, is how we survive ...*

"Quite right," the ancestor nodded.

*Then a voice from above, who gave me hope ...*

"Your second spirit, of far-seeing and love,

helping you to help others

find a way out of grief."

"And of being here now—being able to sing!"

sang Little Feather brightly, out loud.

"You see," said Wise Wing. "You haven't

forgotten. We might not always feel right, but

we need never be alone."

Little Feather felt embraced.

"I may not ever even know what hit me!"

he cried delightfully.

"It's a start," said Wise Wing, "if you

consider the beginning."

As he did, Little Feather could feel

himself floating,

alive with a feeling of joy.

*Close your eyes, breathe deep, and always remember*

*your very first flight.*

Whose words were these? He felt that he'd known

them, carried on wings through every night.

He recalled when his own first touched the sky.

*How does that feel?* asked the voice from his dreams.

"It makes me feel light…light as a feather!"

*You're ready.*

# EPILOGUE

What gives you joy as a bird?

*I love to fly with my wings stretched wide*

*while I flip and spin and criss-cross the sky*

*I love to watch flowers turn to the sun*

*and their petals up to the rain*

*I love to hop on a branch and sing*

*Twee pudo  Twee pudo  Twee pudo  Twee*

*And being part of a family*

*that loves to wake up to an infinite sky*

*and kiss each cloud that passes by*

"So you know," came that voice from

a long-ago dream,

"to cherish your song, as precious as breath."


The lofty echo then disappeared

with the tree;

and Little Feather found himself alone—


until a soft summer wind

lifted his wing

and carried the lightest little bird back home.

CPSIA information can be obtained
at www.ICGtesting.com
Printed in the USA
LVIC04n2320130816
500082LV00002B/2